W9-BNC-057

ISAAC ASIMOV'S
LIBRARY OF THE UNIVERSE

SPACE GARBAGE

by Isaac Asimov

DELL YEARLING NONFICTION

Published by
Dell Publishing
a division of
Bantam Doubleday Dell Publishing Group, Inc.
666 Fifth Avenue
New York, New York   10103

This edition was first published in the United States and Canada in 1989
by Gareth Stevens, Inc.

The reproduction rights to all photographs and illustrations in this book are controlled
by the individuals or institutions credited on page 32 and may not be reproduced
without their permission.

Technical advisers and consulting editors: Fran Millhouser, Julian Baum, and Francis Reddy

Text copyright © 1989 by Nightfall, Inc.
End matter copyright © 1989 by Gareth Stevens, Inc.
Format copyright © 1989 by Gareth Stevens, Inc.

All rights reserved. No part of this book may be reproduced or transmitted in any form
or by any means, electronic or mechanical, including photocopying, recording, or by
any information storage and retrieval system, without the written permission of the
publisher, except where permitted by law. For information, address Gareth Stevens,
Inc., 1555 North RiverCenter Drive, Suite 201, Milwaukee, Wisconsin   53212, USA.

The trademark Yearling® is registered in the U.S. Patent and Trademark Office.
The trademark Dell® is registered in the U.S. Patent and Trademark Office.

ISBN: 0-440-40444-4

Reprinted by arrangement with Gareth Stevens, Inc.

Printed in the United States of America
September 1991

10 9 8 7 6 5 4 3 2 1

CONTENTS

Nowadays, we have seen planets up close, all the way to distant Neptune. We have mapped Venus through its clouds. We have seen the rings around Neptune and the ice volcanoes on Triton, one of Neptune's moons. We have detected strange objects no one knew anything about until recently: quasars, pulsars, black holes. We have learned amazing facts about how the Universe was born and have some ideas about how it may die. Nothing can be more astonishing and more interesting.

We have actually explored our Solar system, especially the part very close to Earth. We have sent many, many rockets into space, most of which continue to orbit Earth even after they stop working. The result is that nearby space is filled with space debris — or "space garbage," as some people call it. In this book, we will take a look at space garbage and consider why it is important.

Isaac Asimov

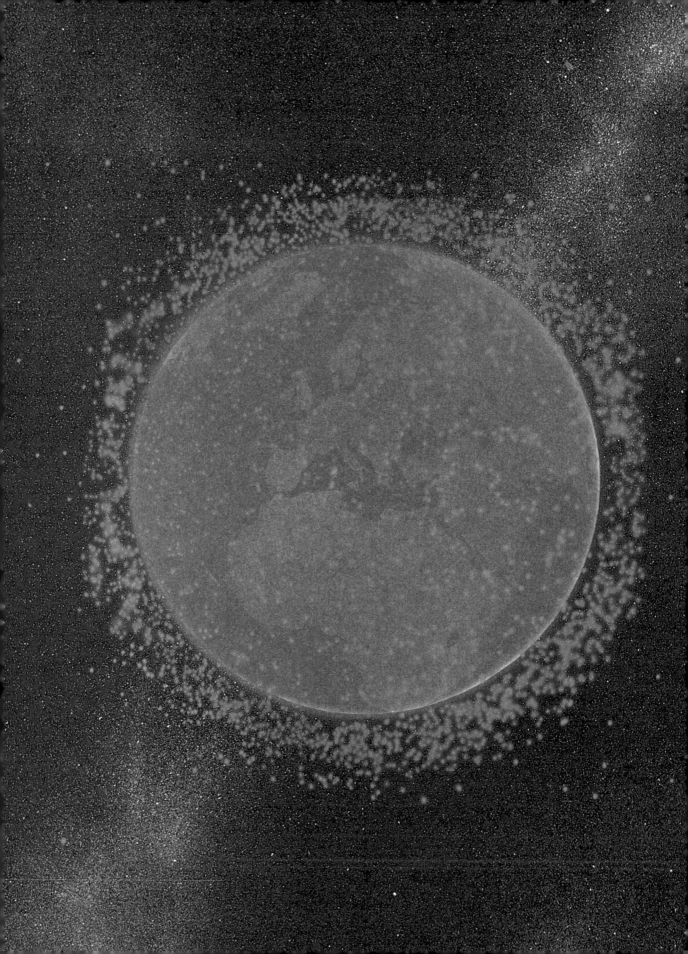

Earth's Orbital Junkyard

We have placed many satellites in orbit about Earth since the late 1950s. Most of them are still circling our planet, even if they're no longer working. At least 80 satellites have broken up into fragments. With time, the fragments break up further. There are now more than 40,000 pieces of space debris at least the size of a golf ball circling Earth.

There are billions of tinier pieces, like small specks of paint. Some debris eventually floats down to Earth, but more is being formed than settles down, and the total amount of "space junk" is steadily increasing.

Satellites and orbital debris swarm around Earth in record numbers. Opposite: This artist's conception is based on a computer image of objects tracked close to our planet.

Below: Thin rings of debris also orbit Earth farther out in space, beyond the "ball" of debris clustered closer to our planet. A NASA computer made this picture.

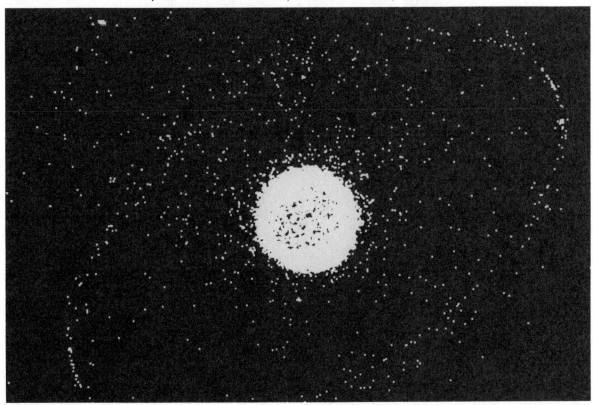

Traces on Other Worlds — A Monument or a Mess?

Spacecraft have also landed on the Moon, and 12 human beings have walked on its soil. Parts of the spacecraft have been left behind, and sites on the Moon have been littered. There are also several spacecraft on Mars and on Venus. The Soviet Union recently launched a probe designed to land equipment on the Martian satellite Phobos.

This means we will have placed material on four different worlds. Some of it may be looked on as monuments to Earth's space programs — the United States flags and plaques on the Moon, for instance. But lots of it is really junk.

Each of the Apollo Moon missions left behind scientific packages, including instruments that watch for "Moon quakes" and mirrors that reflect laser beams from Earth.

Above: a small memorial to the US astronauts and Soviet cosmonauts who gave their lives in the cause of exploring space, left on the Moon by Apollo 15 astronauts.

Left: gold replica of the olive branch brought to the Moon aboard Apollo 11 — a symbol of peace.

Lunar litter — the last trace of humanity?

Suppose that a nuclear war wipes out humanity. Gradually wind, water, and remaining forms of life will destroy what is left of our cities. If visitors from some other civilization come millions of years later, they may find no sign that humanity ever ruled Earth. But on the Moon, there will still be the litter our astronauts left behind between 1969 and 1972, looking almost as it did to begin with. That "junk" may then be our final monument.

Further Frontiers — Hunks of Junk in the Cosmos

We will continue exploring space. There seems to be no doubt about that. But it also seems that we human beings can't go anywhere without leaving behind some of the materials we have produced. On Earth, we have filled the land surfaces with garbage; we have polluted the oceans with all kinds of waste, and we are filling the atmosphere with dust and poisonous gases.

Are we gradually going to pollute space and neighboring worlds, too? And will we continue to do so as we explore further? Will we leave traces of ourselves wherever we go? And will these traces be in the form of useless and unsightly junk?

Above: Time to take out the trash! Astronauts aboard the US Skylab space station pack up their garbage.

Below: a garbage barge carrying its cargo toward the sea. The cars on the bridge give an idea of how big the barge is.

Improperly launched trash bags alarmed cosmonauts on Salyut 6 when they seemed to follow the space station.

Some "space garbage" really is garbage!

In 1978, two cosmonauts in the Soviet Salyut 6 space station dumped two bags of trash into space. Later, ground controllers told the cosmonauts to check out two nearby "unidentified flying objects." One looked out the window — and was shocked to see two dark, round objects keeping pace with the spacecraft! Only after a few hair-raising seconds did he realize that the scary, strange-looking "UFOs" were merely the trash bags they had discarded.

For several nights following the launch of Skylab in 1973, several "extra" satellites streaked across the night sky — parts of the rocket that launched the huge space laboratory.

Left: Radar dishes such as these are part of a worldwide electronic "trash-tracking" network.

From their underground post beneath Cheyenne Mountain in Colorado, members of the US Space Surveillance Center keep track of nearly 7,000 bits of space junk.

Tracking the Trash

Space debris is not just a matter of messiness. It is important to know where it is, especially the big pieces. After all, if we send additional satellites into space, we don't want to put them into an orbit where they will collide with a piece of debris and be put out of action. That is one reason we send radio waves into space — to track the trash.

These radio waves bounce off satellites and debris so that people on Earth know the exact location of each object, whether working or dead, and where it is going. This helps us choose a good orbit for the next satellite.

But one day soon, we just may run out of safe orbits!

Spacewalking — Is It Safe?

Space contains speeding meteoroids, most of them the size of a grain of sand. They move at many miles a second, and even a small one can puncture a spacesuit and kill an astronaut. But space is vast, and so far no "killer meteoroid" has struck any astronaut.

Space debris is equally dangerous. A fleck of paint struck a space shuttle in 1983 and chipped the windshield, which had to be replaced at a cost of $50,000. A slightly larger object might have punctured the windshield and killed the entire crew. The more debris we put up there, the greater the danger.

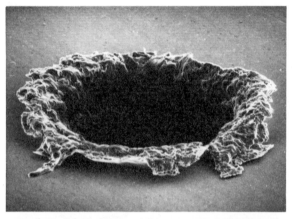

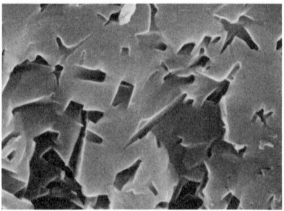

Top: Microscopic craters like this were found on the Solar Maximum satellite after its return to Earth in 1984. High-speed flakes of paint did all the damage!

Bottom: Atomic particles streaming from the Sun leave their marks in Moon rocks. Earth's atmosphere protects us from these particles.

Opposite: A tiny fleck of paint made this microscopic crater in a space shuttle's window — a potentially dangerous cosmic encounter.

Solar wind — another kind of debris

The Sun is always hurling out its own "debris" — electrically charged subatomic particles. This is called the solar wind. The radiation is harmful, though not enough to threaten astronauts. But every once in a while, there is an explosion on the Sun called a solar flare. Then the number of particles rises to a deadly level. There was an enormous flare in 1972 between the two Moon missions. Luckily, there were no astronauts in space at the time.

Satellites — Debris We Depend On

We could stop leaving debris if we stopped sending up satellites, but we really can't do that. Since we began sending them up in the 1950s, we have come to depend on satellites. For instance, some satellites help us predict the weather, tell us about Earth's cloud cover, and track storms such as hurricanes.

Some satellites make it possible for us to send messages across oceans. Some allow ships to know exactly where they are at all times. Some make it possible for us to study Earth, its soil, its oceans, its crops.

We must have satellites, and so we'll continue to end up with their debris.

Above: This orbiting "crystal ball," LAGEOS, may one day help us predict earthquakes. Scientists bounce laser beams off its hundreds of reflectors to measure movements in Earth's crust.

Right: The European Infrared Space Observatory (ISO) will measure the heat of newborn stars.

Satellites are our "eyes in the sky," providing us with a way to see the weather all around our planet. Weather-watching satellites (left) have saved many lives by letting us see how dangerous storms, such as Hurricane Juan (below), develop and move.

What If . . . ? — Skylab and Other Near Misses

Space debris can even be dangerous to us here on Earth. As debris passes through thin wisps of upper air, it gradually comes close to Earth and finally enters the main atmosphere. Small pieces just burn up. But large pieces can reach Earth's surface. Nearly three-quarters of them will splash into the ocean, but some may hit land. Parts of a Soviet satellite, Cosmos 954, fell on northern Canada in 1978.

Also in 1978, increased activity on the surface of the Sun heated up Earth's atmosphere, causing it to expand. This increased the atmosphere's "drag" on the US Skylab satellite, until parts of Skylab finally came down on July 11, 1979, hitting western Australia. It's not very likely that pieces of satellites will hit buildings or people. But someday a lump of debris may do just that.

A plume of gas rises above the Sun's surface. This kind of activity can expand Earth's atmosphere — and bring down satellites in low orbits.

Opposite, left: Cosmos 954, a Soviet satellite that fell on Canada in 1978, scattered radioactive debris that had to be located and removed.

Opposite, right: part of a water tank recovered when Skylab broke apart in Earth's atmosphere.

Only about 30% of Earth's surface is land, and only about 1% of this land has large concentrations of people. So if a large piece of debris falls to Earth, the chances are about 1 in 333 that it might do serious harm to human beings. This means that if a large piece of space debris falls to Earth only once every 10 years, then the odds are that it will be some 3,000 years or more before a piece causes serious harm to people on Earth.

Of course, by bad luck, a piece might hit next year. As our planet's population goes up and cities spread outward, the chances for damage or harm increase. On the other hand, if we clean up space, the chances will decrease. It's that simple.

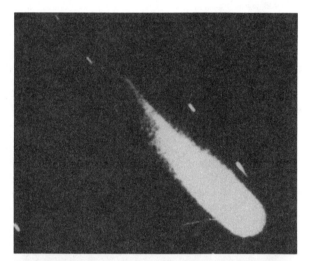

Opposite: the Skylab Orbiting Workshop, launched by the US in 1973.

Left: Satellites that fall to Earth burn and break apart in our atmosphere. Natural space debris also leave glowing trails as they streak to Earth as meteors.

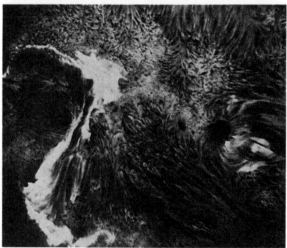

Above: The bright plume of a solar flare leaps above the Sun's surface.

Solar flares — life-and-death questions remain

The explosions on the Sun that expel a deadly tide of charged particles take place at odd times. Scientists don't always know what causes these solar flares or when they'll take place. This means that astronauts working on a space station, for instance, will never know when to expect these dangerous events — so the station will have to be shielded at all times. After further study, flares may become predictable, and life in space will become safer. •

Left: A robot explorer on Mars awaits an oncoming dust storm.

Below: After centuries of Martian erosion, a half-buried Viking lander shows its age.

Cosmic Litter — Will It Last Forever?

Much of the debris in nearby space will return harmlessly to Earth. In this way, nearby space is "self-cleaning." Farther from Earth, space also cleans up after us. The probes that have landed on Venus will be exposed to very high temperatures and the action of strong winds, and they will eventually be reduced to dust. On Mars, sandstorms might do the same, but more slowly.

But on places like our Moon and Phobos, there is no atmosphere to wear down our litter. On these worlds, any junk left behind could last for millions of years. So it is important to remember that under some conditions, our junk may be around forever.

Of course, if we set up a permanent lunar base, we can at least keep the Moon clean. But what about the other litter we leave in the cosmos? It's bound to add up!

A Soviet Venera probe rests on the surface of Venus. The probe stopped transmitting an hour after landing, its electronics destroyed by the planet's tremendous heat.

Cosmic rays — the debris of a dying star?

Cosmic ray particles are more penetrating and deadly than solar wind particles. Usually there are not enough to be dangerous. Astronomers think many originate with supernovas, or violently exploding stars. A nearby supernova may make space deadly for a while. Stars do not explode as supernovas often, and only a few stars are close enough to be dangerous! But a supernova explosion is unpredictable, so we don't know just when danger might come.

Low orbits are the most littered with space junk. Perhaps one day orbiting "garbage collectors" will be used to clean up these trash-filled orbits.

Learning to Keep Space Clean

If we let too much debris accumulate around our planet, it might be impossible for us to find safe orbits for future satellites. One of the tasks of some space shuttle missions is to pick up satellites that aren't working and repair them or remove them. A 1989 shuttle mission successfully picked up the Long Duration Exposure Facility satellite, which had been in orbit since 1984 exposing various materials to the space environment.

We will have to learn to send up satellites that don't easily fall apart into fragments and that survive collisions with fragments already in space. Perhaps we will figure out a way to sweep up the larger pieces.

A black hole — the ultimate trash-masher. Advanced space civilizations may use "small" black holes to dispose of their junk.

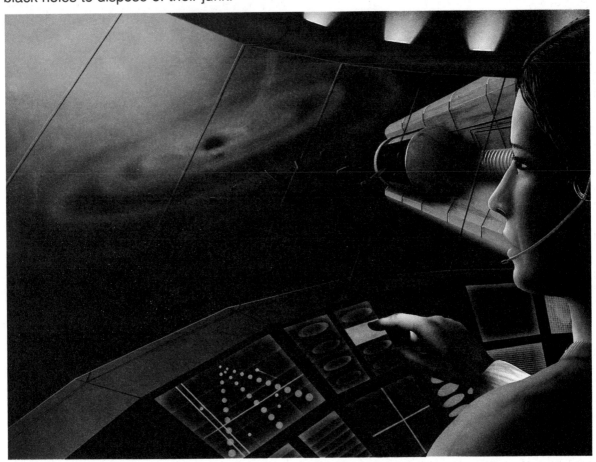

Beyond the Solar System

In 1957, we sent up Sputnik 1, Earth's first artificial satellite. That wasn't so long ago. But today we have sent space probes out beyond the planets. The Pioneer 10 probe is now moving far beyond the known Solar system and is still sending back messages. It could do so until after the year 2000, but eventually its energy will run out and it will stop working. It will continue moving outward, however, as a far-flung piece of junk.

Other probes will follow, and one day there might be large numbers of such dead objects sailing through interstellar space for countless millions of years. Of what value will these objects be during their endless journey into the cosmos?

Opposite: Earth's deep-space probes sail beyond the outer reaches of our Solar system. This artist's concept shows Voyager 2 (foreground), with Pioneer 10 and 11 off to the right. Also shown (background) is the path of Voyager 1, which passed through the plane of Saturn's rings at a steep angle and headed "up" and away from the Solar system.

Skimming the stars

Where are the deep-space probes headed? One of them, Voyager 2, continues to move outward after taking pictures of Uranus in 1986 and of Neptune in 1989. In about 40,000 years, it will skim by a red dwarf star named Ross 248 and be only 1.65 light-years from it. That's still almost 10 trillion miles (16 trillion km) — not very close! But it's the closest Voyager 2 will come to any star other than our Sun in the first million years of its journey.

Above: The time is 100 million years from now. The place is somewhere in interstellar space. Voyager 2, now a derelict craft cratered by the impact of countless tiny meteoroids, drifts in the vicinity of a red supergiant star.

Right: This plaque aboard Pioneer 10 includes images of a woman and a man (the man's hand raised in a sign of good will). A diagram of the Solar system shows Pioneer leaving Earth, flying by Mars and Jupiter, and sailing into interstellar space.

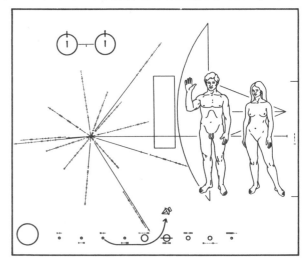

And Finally . . .

Some deep-space probes carry with them plaques giving information about Earth and its location. Some carry records with various sounds on them, including the sounds of humans speaking. The idea behind this is that someday — perhaps millions of years from now — intelligent beings from other worlds may come across such distant debris and discover the plaques and records.

Will it be dangerous to attract their attention? Probably not; there's no reason to think that intelligent beings from distant planets will be unfriendly.

Perhaps even future human beings living in settlements in distant space may discover the plaques and records. Will they be able to understand the information sent out so many millions of years ago? Or will they be so distant from Earth in time and space that they will wonder how beings so much like them could have lived on such a "strange" planet like Earth?

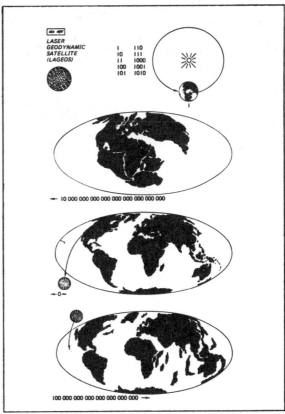

Right: A plaque aboard LAGEOS (see page 14) shows three views of Earth's shifting continents: one of the distant past; one of the present; and one of the distant future.

Fact File: Not All "Space Garbage" Is Garbage!

Like many other things, much of what we send into space — or what comes our way from space — can be good or bad. Satellites can help warn us about dangerous storms. But they can be dangerous themselves when pieces of them fall to Earth. In the same way, meteorites might cause damage on Earth if they fall in the wrong place, but meteorites can also help us learn more about the Universe. Here are some benefits and dangers of different kinds of "space garbage."

A meteoroid hits Earth's atmosphere.

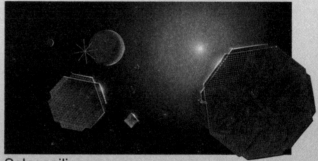

Solar sailing.

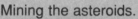

Mining the asteroids.

Kind of "Space Garbage"
Meteoroids, meteorites, and asteroids
Piloted spacecraft
Satellites
Solar wind and solar flares
Strategic Defense Initiative ("Star Wars") antinuclear satellite system
Unpiloted space probes (Hubble Space Telescope, Pioneer, Mariner, Voyager, etc.)

"Star Wars" satellites intercept nuclear warheads.

Good Points	Bad Points
May contain substances that help us learn more about the Universe and the origin of life	May be dangerous if they hit Earth's surface or piloted spacecraft
Enable humans to explore space firsthand, repair satellites or return them to Earth if they are in danger of falling; first step to human colonies in space	Space travel still extremely expensive and dangerous; larger craft orbiting Earth, like Skylab, can be dangerous when they fall out of orbit
Vital for purposes of navigation, modern communication, weather forecasting, national defense, and space exploration	Expensive; can malfunction; increasing number of satellites increases problems and dangers of space debris
Possible future source of energy for Earth and for propelling future spacecraft	Danger to space travelers; danger to humans on Earth if damage to atmosphere continues; disruptive to Earth communication
Possible way of eliminating threat of nuclear war	High cost; might not work; malfunction might send weapons into space, even cause "accidental" war
Safe way of exploring and learning about the Universe; can go to places that no human can safely go, like the surface of Venus — or the outer Solar system and beyond; can help us learn things about space we could not learn from Earth	Individual probes can be expensive and take a long time to develop; launch rockets can leave debris that can fall to Earth; probes take long time to travel to places where they can send us information we want

More Books About Space Garbage

Here are more books that contain information about space debris and other celestial objects in our Solar system. If you are interested in them, check your library or bookstore.

Artificial Satellites. Bendick (Franklin Watts)
The Asteroids. Asimov (Gareth Stevens)
Comets and Meteors. Asimov (Gareth Stevens)
Comets and Meteors. Couper (Franklin Watts)
Comets, Meteors and Asteroids: Rocks in Space. Darling (Dillon)
How Do You Go to the Bathroom in Space? Pogue (TOR Books)
Our Solar System. Asimov (Gareth Stevens)
Rockets, Probes, and Satellites. Asimov (Gareth Stevens)
Voyager: The Story of a Space Mission. Poynter & Lane (Atheneum)

Places to Visit

You can explore outer space — including the places close to our planet where space litter is becoming more and more of a problem — without leaving Earth. Here are some museums and centers where you can find a variety of space exhibits.

Museum of Science and Industry
Chicago, Illinois

London Children's Science Museum
London, Ontario

National Air and Space Museum
Smithsonian Institution
Washington, DC

The Space and Rocket Center
Huntsville, Alabama

Touch the Universe
Manitoba Planetarium
Winnipeg, Manitoba

Calgary Centennial Planetarium
Calgary, Alberta

For More Information About Space Garbage

Here are some places you can write to for more information about the things we put up in space — many of which may contribute to, or help us solve, the problem of space trash. Be sure to tell them exactly what you want to know about or see. Remember to include your age, full name, and address.

For information about space debris and other astronomical matters:

National Space Society
600 Maryland Avenue SW
Washington, DC 20024

Space Communications Branch
Ministry of State for Science and Technology
240 Sparks Street, C. D. Howe Building
Ottawa, Ontario K1A 1A1, Canada

About planetary missions:
NASA Jet Propulsion Laboratory
Public Affairs 180-201
4800 Oak Grove Drive
Pasadena, California 91109

About Strategic Defense Initiative (SDI, "Star Wars"):
Assistant Secretary of Defense for Public Affairs
Public Correspondence Branch, Room 2E777
Pentagon
Washington, DC 20301

Glossary

atmosphere: the gases that surround a planet, star, or moon.

billion: in this book, the number represented by 1 followed by nine zeroes — 1,000,000,000. In some places, such as the United Kingdom (Britain), this number is called "a thousand million." In these places, one billion would then be represented by 1 followed by *12* zeroes — 1,000,000,000,000: a million million, known as a trillion in North America.

black hole: an object in space caused by the explosion and collapse of a star. This object is so tightly packed that not even light can escape the force of its gravity.

cosmic ray particles: subatomic particles arriving from outer space. Our Sun emits some cosmic ray particles when it has large solar flares. Astronomers suspect that supernova explosions are probably responsible for many cosmic ray particles.

cosmonaut: an astronaut, especially one from the Soviet Union.

interstellar: between or among the stars.

light-year: the distance that light travels in one year — nearly six trillion miles (9.6 trillion km).

meteoroid: a lump of rock or metal drifting through space. Meteoroids can be as big as asteroids or as small as specks of dust.

orbit: the path that one celestial object or satellite follows as it circles around another object in space.

pollute: to dirty air, land, water, or space.

probe: a craft that travels in space, photographing celestial bodies and even landing on some of them.

pulsar: a star with all the mass of an ordinary large star but with that mass squeezed into a small ball. It sends out rapid pulses of light or electrical waves.

quasar: a "quasi-stellar," or "star-like," core of a galaxy that may have a large black hole at its center.

radio waves: electromagnetic waves that can be detected by radio receiving equipment.

red dwarf star: a cool, faint star, smaller than our Sun. Red dwarfs are probably the most numerous stars in our Galaxy, but they are so faint that they are very difficult to see.

satellite: a smaller body orbiting a larger body. The Moon is the Earth's <u>natural</u> satellite. Sputnik 1 and 2 were Earth's first <u>artificial</u> satellites.

Skylab: a US research satellite launched in 1973. Three separate crews lived and worked on Skylab until 1974. Skylab itself reentered Earth's atmosphere and came down in 1979.

solar flares: huge explosions of intensely heated gases on the Sun that hurl out great energy. They occur near sunspots, the cooler, darker areas of the Sun.

solar wind: tiny particles that travel from the Sun's surface at a speed of about 300 miles (500 km) a second.

space shuttle: a rocket ship that can be used over and over again, since it returns to Earth after completing each mission.

subatomic particles: those particles, such as protons, electrons, and neutrons, that make up atoms.

supernova: the result of a huge star exploding. When a supernova occurs, material from the star is spread through space.

trillion: See definition for *billion*.

UFO: the abbreviation for Unidentified Flying Object.

Index

The publishers wish to thank the following for permission to reproduce copyright material: front cover, p. 22, © Pat Rawlings, 1988; pp. 4, 24, © Julian Baum, 1988; pp. 5, 26 (lower), 28 (lower left), courtesy of NASA; pp. 6, 7 (both), 8 (upper), 12 (both), 13 (inset), 14 (left), 15 (both), 17 (upper right), 18, 27, photographs courtesy of NASA; p. 8 (lower), © Runk/Schoenberger from Grant Heilman; p. 9, © MariLynn Flynn, 1988; p. 10, photograph courtesy of COMSAT; p. 11 (left), © Dennis Milon; p. 11 (right), photograph courtesy of United States Space Command; p. 13 (full page), photograph courtesy of Rockwell International; p. 14 (right), courtesy of European Space Agency; pp. 16-17 (lower), © Jon Pons/courtesy of Del Woods of DayStar Filter Corporation; p. 17 (upper left), photograph courtesy of US Department of Energy; p. 19 (upper), photograph courtesy of US Space Command; p. 19 (lower), National Optical Astronomy Observatories; pp. 20 (upper), 21, © David A. Hardy; p. 20 (lower), © Bruce Bond; p. 23, © Doug McLeod, 1988; p. 26 (upper), © Adolph Schaller, 1988; p. 28 (upper), © Mark Maxwell, 1985; p. 28 (center), © Rick Sternbach; p. 29, Los Alamos National Laboratory.